The Bathro

A FARCE IN

by Gertrude E. Jennings

SAMUEL FRENCH, INC.
45 West 25th Street NEW YORK 10010
7623 Sunset Boulevard HOLLYWOOD 90046
LONDON TORONTO

ISBN 0 573 62037 7 Printed in U.S.A.

THE BATHROOM DOOR

Produced on Monday, January 10, 1916, at the Victoria Palace, London, with the following cast of characters:—

The Young Man	*Mr. Langhorne Burton*
The Young Lady	*Miss Dorothy Bell*
The Elderly Gentleman . .	*Mr. Frank Halden*
The Elderly Lady	*Miss Margaret Murray*
The Prima Donna	*Miss Margaret Halstan*
The Boots	*Mr. Frank Ridley*

Scene.—*A passage on the fourth floor of the Hotel Majestic. The time is 8 a.m.*

N.B.—"The Boots" may be turned into "A Charwoman" if desirable.

"The Bathroom Door" was performed on board "Repulse" during her voyage from South America to England in October, 1925, with the following Cast of Characters :—

THE YOUNG MAN . .	*Mr. Ward Price.*
THE YOUNG LADY . .	*H.R.H. The Prince of Wales*
THE ELDERLY GENTLEMAN	*Lieut. Butler.*
THE ELDERLY LADY . .	*Pay-Lieut.-Comdr. Youle.*
THE PRIMA DONNA . .	*Lieut.-Comdr. Philip.*
THE BOOTS . . .	*The Hon. R. Ward.*

THE BATHROOM DOOR

The Scene is a passage-way running across the stage and set forward. It is 12 *feet in width. Facing the audience are three doors. The first is labelled* 66, *the centre is* BATHROOM, *and the third is* 67. *The doors must open on to the stage, the handles being on the* L. *hand side of doors. The play can be performed with one door only—the bathroom. There is a small red velvet settee between door of bathroom and* 66. *The stage is empty when curtain rises—then a gay whistling is heard, and there enters from* R. *a handsome* YOUNG MAN, *clad in pyjamas, dressing-gown and bedroom slippers—he carries a loofah, and a towel. He walks up to bathroom, tries door, the whistle stops, he turns and exits smartly, the whistle resumed.*

After a moment's pause there enters from L. *the* YOUNG LADY. *She is very pretty and has fair hair. She wears a simple pretty dressing-gown over her night-dress and carries a sponge and towel. She crosses stage, tries door and exits. A short pause, and the door of* 66 *opens, and the* ELDERLY GENTLEMAN *appears; he is red-faced and white-haired and clad in pyjamas and dressing-gown. He, too, tries the door and then returns to his room. The door of* 67 *opens and there emerges very cautiously the* ELDERLY LADY *in a red flannel dressing-gown. Her hair is twisted tight on top of her head and she is not pretty. She advances in a frightened way to the door, then bolts back into her room.*

A pause—enter, preceded by little trills and bursts of song, the PRIMA DONNA, *a very beautiful woman whose peignoir is more wonderful than most people's best tea-gowns. She has on a lace night-cap. She carries sponge bag and towel. She crosses nonchalantly to the door, tries it, gives an exclamation of disgust and exits, singing. In a moment the* OLD GENTLEMAN *enters, the* MIDDLE-AGED LADY *opens her door, comes out, sees the old gentleman, and shuts her door hastily. The* OLD GENTLEMAN *quickly returns to his room. The* YOUNG LADY *enters briskly, tries door, says, "Oh, bother the thing!" and exits. Re-enter the* PRIMA DONNA*; just as she reaches the door the* YOUNG MAN *enters quickly. The* PRIMA DONNA *drops her sponge-bag; he picks it up, and hands it to her.*

PRIMA DONNA. Oh, thank you so much.

YOUNG MAN. Not at all. I'm afraid the bath room is occupied.

PRIMA DONNA. Yes—so tiresome. It's the only one on this floor.

YOUNG MAN. Absurd—in such a big hotel.

PRIMA DONNA. Isn't it? I usually have a suite, but they are all engaged.

YOUNG MAN. Very full, isn't it?

PRIMA DONNA. Very. (*Drops her sponge-bag. He picks it up.*) So much obliged——

YOUNG MAN. A pleasure.

PRIMA DONNA. Oh, thanks. I don't have to carry these things as a rule, but my maid has a toothache.

YOUNG MAN. How trying!

PRIMA DONNA. Isn't it! What a long time this person is! One must be patient, I suppose.

YOUNG MAN. It seems like that. Of course, your turn comes first.

PRIMA DONNA. Oh, really I——! Well, I *should* be glad. My accompanist will be here at nine-thirty. Music is a hard task-master.

YOUNG MAN. Music! Ah, now I know where I have seen you.

PRIMA DONNA. Oh yes?

YOUNG MAN. Everywhere! But your photographs are not—but then photographs never could be——

PRIMA DONNA. Could be what?

YOUNG MAN. Good enough.

PRIMA DONNA. Really! (*Moves* L.)

YOUNG MAN. Was that rude?

PRIMA DONNA. No—it was charming, but not quite the place or time.

YOUNG MAN. Well, if you could name a better?

PRIMA DONNA. Certainly not—I didn't mean that at all. I must go back and wait till this person is done. (*Crosses* L.)

(PRIMA DONNA *stops.*)

YOUNG MAN. I'm afraid I've offended you. It's my terrible frankness. I *have* to say everything I think, and I couldn't help thinking you very beautiful, could I?

PRIMA DONNA. It must be very awkward.

YOUNG MAN. To be beautiful?

PRIMA DONNA. No, having to say everything you think.

YOUNG MAN. Yes, isn't it? I've been like that since I was a baby.

PRIMA DONNA. Still you're grown up now, aren't you?

YOUNG MAN. Oh yes—quite grown up. (*Looking at her with great admiration.*)

(*The* OLD GENTLEMAN'S *door opens.*)

PRIMA DONNA. I must fly. (*Going.*)

YOUNG MAN. I'll keep guard and tell you when this person comes out.

PRIMA DONNA (*off stage*). Oh, please don't trouble.

YOUNG MAN. It's no trouble. (*Darts back to door.*)

(*The* OLD GENTLEMAN *comes up to the door in front of which the* YOUNG MAN *is standing.*)

OLD GENTLEMAN. Excuse me, sir, but if you have quite done with the bathroom, I would like to get in.

YOUNG MAN. I haven't even begun with the bathroom yet, sir.

OLD GENTLEMAN. Oh! You haven't been in?

YOUNG MAN. No such luck.

OLD GENTLEMAN. My apologies.

YOUNG MAN. Not at all.

OLD GENTLEMAN. But you won't mind my pointing out that I came here first?

YOUNG MAN. Pardon me. This is my third effort.

OLD GENTLEMAN. I came at seven-thirty.

YOUNG MAN. I came at seven twenty-five.

OLD GENTLEMAN. There's no record.

YOUNG MAN. No. I didn't leave my card.

OLD GENTLEMAN. I have a very pressing appointment.

YOUNG MAN. But I am keeping the place for a lady.

OLD GENTLEMAN. A lady! That's very unusual.

YOUNG MAN. Not at all. They have baths too, you know, sometimes.

OLD GENTLEMAN. Still, to *engage* a bath——

YOUNG MAN. Why not go to the next floor?

OLD GENTLEMAN. I don't care to.

YOUNG MAN. Just as you like.

(*The* OLD GENTLEMAN *glares at the* YOUNG MAN. *Door of* 67 *opens and the* OLD LADY *comes out into the passage, sees the two men.*)

OLD LADY. Oh!

(*The two men turn and see her. She darts back, leaving a worsted shoe. She bangs the door, the men giggle.*)

YOUNG MAN. Cinderella has left her slipper.

OLD GENTLEMAN. Oughtn't we to return it?

YOUNG MAN. Yes, do. (*Passes him over towards slipper.*)

OLD GENTLEMAN. It's your privilege, as the younger man.

YOUNG MAN. But it was your idea. I couldn't think of interfering.

OLD GENTLEMAN. I can't do it. I never do that sort of thing.

YOUNG MAN. What sort of thing?

OLD GENTLEMAN. You know perfectly well what I meant. Besides, I haven't shaved.

YOUNG MAN. You don't need to shave before you return a slipper.

OLD GENTLEMAN. The lady will think you very impolite.

YOUNG MAN. But she *looked* at *you*.

(*The* OLD GENTLEMAN, *alarmed, makes for his door, turns.*)

OLD GENTLEMAN. If I go I may lose my turn at the bathroom.

YOUNG MAN. But if *I* go, I shall lose the turn of a more beautiful person than either you or I—a being brighter than the stars, more fascinating than a fairy princess.

OLD GENTLEMAN. Oh, I thought you were waiting for *that* lady. (*Pointing at door.*)

YOUNG MAN. Cinderella! Oh dear me, no!

OLD GENTLEMAN. Still, I don't see why the poor soul should go without her shoe.

YOUNG MAN. It's a shame.

OLD GENTLEMAN. When I was a young man I never neglected an opportunity——

YOUNG MAN (*meaningly*). I'm sure you didn't——

(*Enter the* YOUNG LADY *rapidly. She stops abruptly at seeing the men.*)

YOUNG LADY. Oh dear! Is there *still* some one in the bathroom?

YOUNG MAN. I'm afraid there is——

YOUNG LADY. Thanks. I'll go back.

YOUNG MAN. Wouldn't you like to wait here?

YOUNG LADY. Oh no—I'll wait in my room. (*Exits.*)

YOUNG MAN. This *is* a nice hotel!

OLD GENTLEMAN. Is that the star and the fairy princess?

YOUNG MAN. No. But she's very bewitching, isn't she? I expect the star will soon return.

OLD GENTLEMAN. She will? Well, if there's going to be a procession of beautiful ladies I'd better go and shave——

YOUNG MAN. Good luck.

OLD GENTLEMAN. May I trust to your honour that I have the bath next but one?

YOUNG MAN. You may trust anything.

(OLD GENTLEMAN *exits.* YOUNG MAN *goes to slipper.* OLD GENTLEMAN *reopens door.* YOUNG MAN *flies back to bathroom.*)

OLD GENTLEMAN (*at his door*). I still think you ought to return that slipper. (*Laughing.*)

YOUNG MAN. Shut your door and I will.

(*The* OLD GENTLEMAN *shuts his door and the* YOUNG MAN *picks up the slipper, advances to 67, and taps. Pause. He raps louder. The door opens and the* ELDERLY LADY'S *head appears. She screams and shuts the door. Enter the* PRIMA DONNA.)

PRIMA DONNA. Oh!

YOUNG MAN. It's only lost property.

PRIMA DONNA. What a peculiar affair! What is it meant to be? A tea cosy?

YOUNG MAN. It's a slipper.

PRIMA DONNA. Really (*The* YOUNG MAN *hangs*

the slipper on OLD LADY'S *door knob.*) Are you leaving them at *every* door?

YOUNG MAN. No, I——

(*The* OLD GENTLEMAN'S *door opens.* YOUNG MAN *darts to bathroom. The* OLD GENTLEMAN *looks out—he has lathered his face—he darts back at seeing the* PRIMA DONNA.)

PRIMA DONNA (*crossing* R., *indignant*). Is that the person who was all that time bathing?

YOUNG MAN. No. The person is still inside.

PRIMA DONNA (R.C.). What!!

YOUNG MAN (L.C.). It's quite true. I've been guarding the door like Casabianca ever since you left me.

PRIMA DONNA. It's really very selfish to come into a hotel and wallow in baths like this. Don't you think we ought to bang on the door?

YOUNG MAN. But supposing it's a lady?

PRIMA DONNA. That's no reason for being in a bath all the morning.

YOUNG MAN. I don't suppose she'll be more than another twenty minutes. Don't you think you might wait here? The time would pass so quickly!

PRIMA DONNA. The question is, who else would pass?

YOUNG MAN. Does that matter?

PRIMA DONNA. You see in my position one has to be so very careful. I can't help being rather well known, can I?

YOUNG MAN. Don't help it.

PRIMA DONNA. Of course, if my lady secretary or my lady typist were here it would be different.

YOUNG MAN. It wouldn't be half so nice. Don't you think you could sit here just for a moment? Isn't the tea-cosy sufficient chaperone?

PRIMA DONNA. It's very unconventional!

YOUNG MAN. Still the circumstances are unusual.

aren't they? One doesn't often meet beautiful celebrities outside the bathroom door at eight o'clock in the morning.

PRIMA DONNA. I always get up early because I like to take my pet tiger for a walk.

YOUNG MAN. Your what?

PRIMA DONNA. My tiger. He's such a darling. The top of his head is like velvet. When I stroke it I have the most wonderful thrill.

YOUNG MAN (*smoothing his hair*). I wish I were your pet tiger.

PRIMA DONNA. You really shouldn't say that, you know! If my mother were here——!

YOUNG MAN. You'll have the passage full if you go on wishing people were here. Do put down your things just for a moment.

PRIMA DONNA. Well, perhaps for a moment. (*She crosses* L. *and sits. He* R. *of settee, she* L.)

YOUNG MAN. Are you staying in this hotel long?

PRIMA DONNA. Oh no. We go away to-day. I sang here last night—in the Concert Hall, and to-day I go to Bournemouth for another concert.

YOUNG MAN. Bournemouth! Is that a nice place?

PRIMA DONNA. Delightful.

YOUNG MAN. I wish *I* were going to Bournemouth.

PRIMA DONNA. It isn't very far. My chauffeur does it in two hours and a half. But I have to see my doctor on the way. For my throat, you know. We singers have to be so careful. (*Drawing herself a little away from him.*)

YOUNG MAN. You seem to have a great many people looking after you, and no wonder!

PRIMA DONNA. Life is full of pitfalls, isn't it?

YOUNG MAN. Yes—thank Heaven! Are you going to stay long at Bournemouth?

PRIMA DONNA. Only one night.

YOUNG MAN. Where do you go next?

PRIMA DONNA. Southsea.

YOUNG MAN. Is that a nice place?

PRIMA DONNA. I hate it.

YOUNG MAN. Still, I wish I were going to Southsea.

PRIMA DONNA. You are fond of travelling?

YOUNG MAN. Loathe it. (*Gazes at her. She becomes very dignified, rises and crosses* R.)

PRIMA DONNA. I really think we ought to bang on that door.

YOUNG MAN. *Must* we?

PRIMA DONNA. Well, my manicurist is coming at nine and I shall never be ready.

YOUNG MAN. Do you really want to go?

PRIMA DONNA. I really think I ought to.

YOUNG MAN. Think how soon you will be going to Bournemouth?

(*During above,* ELDERLY LADY *opens her door and appears on her hands and knees with an umbrella. She scoops round, searching for her slipper, and at the word "Bournemouth" she catches the* YOUNG MAN'S *ankle. He screams. She drops the umbrella and exits.*)

PRIMA DONNA. There! Some's one's coming!

YOUNG MAN. Coming! They've come! (*He hangs umbrella on door knob.*)

PRIMA DONNA. Please bang!

YOUNG MAN. You mean it?

PRIMA DONNA. Of course.

(YOUNG MAN *sighs and rises reluctantly, taps on the bathroom door very softly with his loofah.*)

PRIMA DONNA. That's not a very big bang.

YOUNG MAN. Well, it's not a very big door.

PRIMA DONNA. Oh, please go on! It's really getting *too* late.

(*The* YOUNG MAN *knocks louder.*)

PRIMA DONNA. Speak. Say something.

YOUNG MAN. But I don't know if it's a him or a her——

PRIMA DONNA. Well, speak to both. You know what I mean.

YOUNG MAN Dear sir or madam, would you kindly oblige me by saying how much longer you require the bathroom?

(*A pause.*)

YOUNG MAN (*louder*). Will you be very much longer, sir? Or madam?

(*A pause.*)

Sir, there are quantities of people requiring the bath, madam.

(*A pause.*)

PRIMA DONNA. No reply?

YOUNG MAN. Not a word!

PRIMA DONNA. No sound of washing?

YOUNG MAN. Not a wash!

PRIMA DONNA (*walking rapidly up and down*). Well, really, you know, isn't it disgraceful? I am not accustomed to this sort of thing. Of course at home I have five bathrooms and a swimming bath. I daresay you've seen it in the papers, and to be kept waiting in a public corridor—don't you think it's insulting? (*Is* L.)

YOUNG MAN (L.C.). Rotten. But of course you can't expect me to be sorry.

PRIMA DONNA. How do you mean?

YOUNG MAN. Don't I owe the great pleasure of meeting you to this mishap?

PRIMA DONNA. Oh! Well——

YOUNG MAN. In fact, I feel the deepest gratitude to this bathing person.

PRIMA DONNA. Still, it must be nearly nine. I think the time has come to get it out, don't you?

YOUNG MAN (*sighing*). I suppose so—but you knew I've done my best.

PRIMA DONNA. Let me try.

YOUNG MAN (*crossing* R.). Yes, you try.

(*She knocks violently on the door.* 66 *opens and the* OLD GENTLEMAN *comes out.*)

(67 *also opens and the* ELDERLY LADY *peeps into the passage. The* OLD GENTLEMAN *comes up. The* YOUNG LADY *enters.*)

YOUNG LADY (L.C.) What *is* happening?

OLD GENTLEMAN (R.). Excuse me, can I help?

YOUNG LADY. Are you trying to get in?

PRIMA DONNA (C.). We're trying to get some one else out.

OLD GENTLEMAN. Great Scott! Is that person still there?

YOUNG LADY. How rotten!

PRIMA DONNA. Disgraceful, isn't it? (*Bangs on door.*) Come out, please, whoever you are! (*The* PRIMA DONNA *listens. Turning on the others.*) It is simply defying me!

YOUNG LADY. Perhaps it's some child who can't unlock the door.

OLD GENTLEMAN. But it would *answer.*

OLD LADY (L., *in a high voice*). Oh, do you think that it can be a lunatic?

PRIMA DONNA (*moving away from the bathroom to* R.). What a very unpleasant idea!

YOUNG MAN (*follows her tenderly*). Don't be alarmed! I will attack it with my loofah.

OLD GENTLEMAN. I 'think if it's a lunatic we ought to fetch the chambermaid.

YOUNG LADY. There's a bell. I'll ring. (*Does so.*)

PRIMA DONNA. But the manager has no business to take in lunatics, especially the kind that shut themselves up in bathrooms.

YOUNG MAN. But we really don't know that it *is* a lunatic.

PRIMA DONNA. Don't you think you might look through the keyhole?

YOUNG MAN. Well, it's a bit awkward, isn't it? I mean—you see—we don't know what's inside.

PRIMA DONNA. Still, the time has come for desperate measures.

YOUNG MAN. No, I'm sorry I can't.

(*The* PRIMA DONNA *shrugs her shoulders and advances to* OLD GENTLEMAN.)

PRIMA DONNA. Would *you* look through the keyhole?

OLD GENTLEMAN. I? Well, I hardly think it's my place. Perhaps that lady would (*pointing to* ELDERLY LADY) look through the keyhole.

OLD LADY. I? Certainly not.

YOUNG LADY. I will. I don't care a dump.

(*She advances. They all make room for her. She kneels down on the floor and looks through keyhole.*)

PRIMA DONNA (R. *of her*). Well, well?

OLD GENTLEMAN (L. *of her*). What do you see?

YOUNG LADY. I *think*——

YOUNG MAN (R.). Yes, yes?

YOUNG LADY. I can't quite——

PRIMA DONNA. Oh, do be quick.

YOUNG LADY. I can't see anything.

OLD GENTLEMAN. Nonsense, my dear young lady.

YOUNG LADY (*rising*). I can't really. There seems to be something dark in front of the keyhole——

PRIMA DONNA. There! It *is* a lunatic preparing to rush out. (*Crosses* L.)

(ELDERLY LADY *returns.*)

YOUNG MAN (*crossing* L.). Don't be frightened! (*Supports* PRIMA DONNA.)

YOUNG LADY (R.C.). What can it be?

OLD LADY. May not some one have swooned inside?

YOUNG MAN. Ah! A very good suggestion. Some one has swooned.

PRIMA DONNA. But they wouldn't swoon standing up, would they?

OLD GENTLEMAN (R.). They may be leaning against the door.

PRIMA DONNA. Why doesn't somebody come. It's really a matter for the manager. Could you ring the bell again?

YOUNG LADY. Rather! (*Rings bell.*)

OLD GENTLEMAN. It's becoming a matter for the police.

OLD GENTLEMAN. Oh! Do you think it's foul play?

PRIMA DONNA. Foul play!

OLD LADY. Or it may be suicide!

PRIMA DONNA. Oh! What an awful idea! What a thing to suggest! Really, that has made me quite terrified!

YOUNG MAN (*crossing to* OLD LADY). You shouldn't have said that, madam.

OLD LADY. I can't help it. I feel it's true—something dark hanging over the door!! What else can it be but suicide?

PRIMA DONNA (*screams. Pushing them aside, she runs to bathroom door*). Ah! It's true! I know it! I have guessed the awful secret!

ALL. What is it?

PRIMA DONNA (*coming down stage* L.). He has committed suicide!

ALL. Who has?

PRIMA DONNA. My husband.

ALL. What!! (OLD LADY *sinks on settee.*)

YOUNG MAN (L. *of her, astounded*). Your *husband*! I didn't even know you were married!!

PRIMA DONNA (*vehemently*). I *told* you I had a husband!

YOUNG MAN. Pardon me, you didn't. You told me you had a swimming bath! You also mentioned a maid, a secretary, a motor car, a chauffeur, a manicurist and a tiger, but you *never* said you had a husband!

PRIMA DONNA. Well, I have, so there!

YOUNG MAN. This is a terrible blow for me.

(*He sits on settee on the* OLD LADY'S *knee, springs up, apologizing.*)

OLD GENTLEMAN. Surely this is not so much a question of whether this lady has a husband as it is whether he has killed himself in the bathroom.

PRIMA DONNA (*violently. He, frightened, backs away*). I *have* got a husband I tell you! I have! And he is there! (*Pointing at bathroom.*)

OLD LADY. Oh! Will somebody ring the bell!

(*They all press towards the bell, except* PRIMA DONNA, *who bursts into tears. She is* R. *of stage.*)

YOUNG MAN (*returns to her*). Oh, *please*! Don't be upset!

OLD GENTLEMAN. Now, my dear madam, what reason have you to think that your husband would make away with himself?

(PRIMA DONNA, YOUNG MAN, OLD GENTLEMAN, YOUNG LADY, OLD LADY.)

PRIMA DONNA. We had quarrelled! We had a terrible quarrel—it was about the tiger! It bites him and he is so terribly sensitive! He said choose between us, and I chose the tiger! He loves me passionately and he rushes off in terrible despair!

OLD GENTLEMAN. When? When?

YOUNG MAN. Where?

PRIMA DONNA. At Kidderminster!

YOUNG MAN. But then he must be in a Kidderminster bathroom?

PRIMA DONNA. No, no. You don't understand! He flew after me to make it up—he took a room in this hotel—he said it was his last night on earth!

OLD LADY. How beautiful! (*All look at her.*)

PRIMA DONNA He has kept his word! He has laid down his life!

OLD GENTLEMAN. Well, I think it was most inconsiderate of him, in our bathroom!

YOUNG MAN. Sir, I must beg you to moderate your language. My dear lady, don't cry, I beseech you. No one could possibly blame you. Of course it's a very dreadful affair, but still you must be brave. You owe a duty to the public. You must think of your voice.

PRIMA DONNA. True, true! I must! Yes, I must forget my private griefs! I have a larger sphere! A greater trust!

(OLD GENTLEMAN *tries to attract* YOUNG MAN'S *attention.*)

YOUNG MAN. Meanwhile rely on me! Everything that I can do is at your service! Command me in everything! (*Kicks* OLD GENTLEMAN.)

PRIMA DONNA. Thank you! How good you are!

OLD GENTLEMAN (*testily*). That's all very well, but something must be done! The manager must be called!

YOUNG MAN. Well, call him!

YOUNG LADY. Why doesn't somebody answer the bell?

OLD GENTLEMAN (*to* ELDERLY LADY). Madam, will you kindly call over the stairs?

OLD LADY. Oh no! I might be seen.

YOUNG LADY. I'll call. I don't mind being seen. (*She runs off* L.)

OLD LADY. I'll ring the bell in my room.

OLD GENTLEMAN. I'll help you (*following her*).

OLD LADY. No, no! (*Exits.*)

OLD GENTLEMAN. I'll ring all the bells in the house. (*Exits* R.)

PRIMA DONNA. Oh! My kind friend, what a tragedy! Look! How my hand trembles!

YOUNG MAN (*taking it*). It does indeed. There,

there! Don't cry any more! After all, he has treated you very badly.

PRIMA DONNA. Yes, he has, hasn't he? He wasn't always very kind. He never understood me. He was of the *world*, you know. I flew upward, but he dragged me down.

YOUNG MAN. I'm afraid you weren't very happy.

PRIMA DONNA. Not very. Mine is such a loving nature——

YOUNG MAN. Yes, yes!

PRIMA DONNA. I only ask for sympathy, a little sympathy—a little love.

YOUNG MAN. And a little tiger.

PRIMA DONNA. What did you say?

YOUNG MAN. Nothing. Don't you think that some day far, far distant, you might find another soul more in tune with yours?

PRIMA DONNA. Ah, what a beautiful dream! But my kind, kind friend! What may I call you?

YOUNG LADY (*off stage. Very shrilly*). Boots! (*They separate.*)

YOUNG MAN. Who said boots?

(*Enter* OLD GENTLEMAN *and* ELDERLY LADY.)

OLD GENTLEMAN. } Has she found any one?
OLD LADY. } The bells are quite useless.

(*Enter* YOUNG LADY.)

YOUNG LADY. It's all right! Some one's come at last.

OLD GENTLEMAN. Is it the manager?

YOUNG LADY. No, it's the boots.

PRIMA DONNA. The boots! To send the boots at such a moment!

YOUNG LADY. Here he comes! (L.)

(*Enter* BOOTS. *He is very taciturn.*)

BOOTS. Wot's up?

OLD GENTLEMAN (R.) What's up! That's no

way to talk. Here we're ringing bells and shouting like mad——

BOOTS. That bell's broke.

PRIMA DONNA (R.C.). Broke!

OLD LADY. Disgraceful!

YOUNG MAN (*crossing to him*). Look here, my man, there's been an accident. This lady's husband has—is——

(PRIMA DONNA *sobs.*)

Well, he's in the bathroom——

BOOTS. That ain't an accident!

(YOUNG MAN *returns* R., *disgusted.*)

PRIMA DONNA (*crossing to* BOOTS). Miserable boy! Fetch the manager at once! Bid him tell the world that for love of me my husband has perished.

BOOTS. 'Ow do you know 'e's perished?

PRIMA DONNA. He has been in that bathroom silent, for hours, and the door—the door is locked.

BOOTS. Oh, I know that there door. Goes like that sometimes. That ain't locked. Look 'ere!

(*He opens the door. They crowd to look in at the bathroom. All exclaim.*)

ALL. It is open!

(PRIMA DONNA *enters bathroom, reappears at door.*)

PRIMA DONNA. It is empty! (*Dramatically to* BOOTS.) Where then is the body of my husband?

BOOTS (*callous*). It's downstairs 'aving its breakfast——

(*All exclaim as the curtain descends rapidly. For call the* OLD GENTLEMAN *is seen entering the bathroom. He shuts door. The four others rush to door and bang on it, while the* BOOTS *exits whistling.*)

(CURTAIN.)

Other Publications for Your Interest

A GALWAY GIRL

(ALL GROUPS—DRAMA)

By GERALDINE ARON

1 man, 1 woman—Interior

A married couple, seated at opposite ends of a table, reminisce about their life together Each presents the situation from his or her point of view, rarely addressing each other directly. The characters are young to begin with, then middle-aged, then old, then one of them dies. The anecdotes they relate are both humorous and tragic. Their lives seem wasted, yet at the end the wife's muted gesture of affection conveys the love that can endure through years of household bickering and incompatibility. A critical success in London, Ireland and the author's native South Africa. "A very remarkable play."—Times Literary Supplement, London. "A touching account of two wasted lives."—Daily Telegraph, London. "A minute tapestry cross-stitched with rich detail—invested with a strong strain of uncomfortable truths."—The Irish Times, Dublin.

TWO PART HARMONY

(PLAY)

By KATHARINE LONG

1 man, 1 woman—Interior

A play about a confrontation of wits between an alert, pre-adolescent girl and a mentally unsettled child-man. On a spring morning in 1959, eight year old Jessie Corington, home alone on a sick day from school, receives an unexpected visit from Hank Everett, a former friend of the family who used to look like Bobby Darin. From the moment he arrives, Hank's eccentric behavior challenges Jessie's cherished belief in adult maturity. Gradually, however, she welcomes her new found playmate and becomes entranced as he enlists her aid in a telephone search for his estranged wife. As the play builds, their bond of friendship is almost shattered when the violence beneath Hank's innocence surfaces against his will. "The work of an artist skilled in deft, understated draughtmanship."—Village Voice.